Mysterious Encounters

Urban Legends

by Rachel Lynette

KIDHAVEN PRESS
A part of Gale, Cengage Learning

Detroit • New York • San Francisco • New Haven, Conn • Waterville, Maine • London

LIBRARY OF CONGRESS CATALOGING-IN-PUBLICATION DATA

Lynette, Rachel.
Urban legends / by Rachel Lynette.
p. cm. — (Mysterious encounters)
Includes bibliographical references and index.
ISBN 978-0-7377-4049-3 (hardcover)
1. Urban folklore. I. Title.
GR78.L96 2008
398.2091732—dc22 2008009551

KidHaven Press
27500 Drake Rd.
Farmington Hills, MI 48331

ISBN-13: 978-0-7377-4049-3
ISBN-10: 0-7377-4049-3

Printed in the United States of America
2 3 4 5 6 7 12 11 10 09 08

Contents

Chapter 1
True Story! 4

Chapter 2
Animal Antics 13

Chapter 3
Frightening Food 23

Chapter 4
Strange and Bizarre 33

Notes 41
Glossary 42
For Further Exploration 44
Index 46
Picture Credits 48
About the Author 48

Chapter 1

True Story!

"Did you hear about that old lady who put her cat in the microwave?"

"Are you sure you want to eat that? My brother's friend's dad once bit into a drumstick like that and it turned out to be a fried rat!"

These are the beginnings of two well-known urban legends. Urban legends are short stories that are passed from person to person. They tend to be bizarre, funny, or horrific, and they often have an unexpected twist. These stories are always assumed to be true, though they rarely are. When people tell these stories, they are never about themselves or even someone they know. Often they are about a person someone they know knows—or to put it more clearly, a friend of a friend. For example, an urban legend might start, "My sister's friend was in a store when. . . ."

Urban legends generally cannot be traced to their original source. They may come from true events that have been altered, celebrity gossip, the Internet, or even old folktales. As the story is passed

The tale of a mishap involving an old lady who accidentally cooks her pet in a microwave oven like this one is a common urban legend.

from person to person, the details change. Soon there are many versions of the same story. For example, in the urban legend about the old woman who puts her poodle in the microwave, it is not always a poodle that comes to an explosive end. Sometimes the story involves an expensive Persian cat or even her grandson's pet hamster. Before microwaves were invented, a similar urban legend involved an elderly woman who puts her beloved cat in the oven to dry it off after it was caught in a rainstorm. Unfortunately, she accidentally turns the oven to broil and cooks the cat to a crisp. In another version, it was a clothes dryer that killed that cat. Thankfully, like most urban legends, this one has never been proved to be a true story.

What Are Urban Legends About?

Most urban legends involve ordinary people doing ordinary things that somehow go terribly wrong. Part of the appeal of an urban legend is that it seems like it could happen to anyone—man, woman, or child. In some cases, bad things happen to innocent people who have no reason to think that anything bad would happen to them. The man who bites into a rat instead of a chicken drumstick is a good example. But sometimes the story shows how a person gets exactly what they deserve. For example, in another urban legend about dining out, a customer is extremely rude to the waitress. The waitress gets her revenge by secretly spitting in his soda.

Warning

Some urban legends serve as warnings. By showing the consequences of risky or foolish behavior, they may convince someone who is considering doing something similar to reconsider.

Urban legends related to food are popular. This may be because everyone can relate to accidentally eating something awful. There are also many urban legends about animals. Some of these stories involve a person doing something cruel to an animal. In others a person makes poor choices around an animal that result in property damage, injury, or even death. In one well-known urban legend, a father smears honey on his child's face in order to get a cute picture of a bear licking her face. In the story, which is not true, the bear eats the child along with the honey.

People doing foolish things show up in many urban legends. But sometimes the stories involve people doing especially clever things. For example, in one story a man finds a smart way to dispose of his garbage during a sanitation **strike**. Each day he wraps his garbage up like a gift. He puts the gift-wrapped package in the front seat of his car, drives to a busy

A thief tempted to steal a gift left in a parked car may think twice upon hearing the urban legend about a man who wrapped his garbage like a present, hoping it would be stolen, in order to dispose of it during a sanitation strike.

area, and leaves the car doors unlocked. When he returns to his car, the "gift" has been stolen.

What Is the Appeal?

Urban legends are a part of the way people communicate with each other. Like talking about sports or the weather at a party, people often use urban legends to make others laugh or to help people to feel at ease. Everyone loves to hear a good story, and for many people telling one is even more fun. Passing around urban legends helps bring people together.

Urban legends appeal to human nature. In many urban legends, mean people are punished and kind people are rewarded. This can have the effect of making people feel that the world is a fair place where everyone gets what they deserve—a comforting thought to most people. When a story tells of a clever person who finds a way to "beat the system," those who hear the story can admire the person, maybe even relate to him or her. When someone does something foolish in an urban legend, people can assure themselves that they would never do anything so stupid. In many ways urban legends help people to feel better about the world they live in and about themselves.

Borrowing Material

Urban legends sometimes show up as part of the plot on TV shows. Sitcoms may use stories about something getting mixed up or someone ending up in an embarrassing situation, while shows like the *X Files* have used scary urban legends for material.

Bizarre urban legends are appealing not only because they are interesting, but also because no matter how unlikely the story, it still *could* have happened. For example, in one well-known urban legend, a woman uses highly **flammable** bug-killing spray to kill a cockroach in the toilet. Later, her hus-

Urban legends tend to involve unlikely but nevertheless possible situations, such as that of the man who accidentally started a fire like this one in his bathroom with the toss of a match after (unbeknownst to him) his wife sprayed a cockroach inside the toilet with bug killer.

band decides to smoke a cigarette while using the bathroom. He throws the match into the toilet, which explodes and leaves him with burns on sensitive parts of his body. Each part of the story is unremarkable—killing a bug, the bug spray being flammable, smoking in the bathroom. It is when they are put together that the story becomes interesting.

Are They True?

Most urban legends are not true stories, although many of them contain elements that are based on truth. For example, in one urban legend, a girl with a complex hairstyle is thought to have a colony of spiders living in her hair. In some versions she dies from being bitten by one of them. In the 1960s many hairstyles involved ratted hair, which was piled high on the head and held there with large amounts of hairspray. One style was even called a beehive. Girls often did not wash their hair for days or even weeks to keep their hairdos together. But there have been no known cases of spiders actually living in someone's hair.

Some urban legends also have parts that appear in ancient legends and folktales. In one story a man leaves a construction site each day with a wheelbarrow full of dirt. The construction site guard digs through the dirt every day, convinced that the man must be stealing something, but all he ever finds is dirt. It is only years later that the man confesses he was actually stealing wheelbarrows.

Lots of teasing and hairspray make it impossible to wash a beehive hairdo like the one worn by this woman without ruining it, but it's still unlikely that spiders would make nests inside of one, as one urban legend claims.

This urban legend comes from a Turkish folktale about the trickster Nasradin, who steals donkeys by loading them up with pots and pans.

In most cases, an urban legend cannot be traced to its source, so unless it can be proved that it is physically impossible, there is no way to know for sure whether it is true or not. Maybe a man really did bite into a fried rat, and perhaps an elderly woman really did put her dog in the microwave. When it comes right down to it, no one knows for sure.

Animal Antics

Animals are often the subject of urban legends. Sometimes these animals are pets. Other times they are more exotic creatures, like snakes or alligators. Insects are particularly popular in these stories.

The Exploding Cactus

In this urban legend, a man buys an expensive, 3-foot (91cm) potted cactus. A few weeks later, he notices that the cactus is moving. He decides to call a plant expert. When the expert hears his story, he tells the man to leave his house immediately and wait outside for help to come.

Help comes in the form of two fire trucks, a police car, and an ambulance. A man wearing a large amount of protective gear and holding a flamethrower drags the cactus outside. He then fires up the flamethrower and torches the cactus. The owner, now completely confused, is not allowed to get near the cactus until it is burned to a crisp. When he finally gets a closer look, he finds a pile of burned, plate-size **tarantula** spiders. According

Although the wild story of a man who bought a cactus for his home, only to find it infested with tarantulas similar to this one, is an oft-told urban legend. It is most definitely not true: there is no breed of the large spider that lays eggs inside of cacti.

to the plant expert, this breed of tarantula lays its eggs inside a cactus. The eggs hatch and the spiders grow. Eventually they grow so big that they pop out of the cactus, literally causing it to explode.

This story has several versions. Sometimes the spiders are scorpions. Sometimes the person does not call anyone and the cactus explodes, spewing tarantulas everywhere. These legends often end with a trip to the hospital.

Fortunately, this could never really happen. There is no breed of tarantula that lays its eggs in cacti. Also, it would take more than a year for tarantula babies to get even close to plate-size.

The Mexican Pet

Another well-known story is that of the Mexican "dog." In this story a woman is vacationing in Mexico. While in a large Mexican city, she sees a small, mangy dog. She feels sorry for the stray and gives it some of her lunch. The dog follows her through the streets for the rest of the day. She thinks this dog is so adorable that she decides to adopt it. She brings it back to her hotel and even shares her bed with it. Once she returns to the United States, she takes her new pet to a vet to get its shots. After examining the animal, the vet asks the woman if she has ever heard the dog bark. The woman replies that she has not, but sometimes it makes a squeaking noise. The vet then informs the woman that her new "dog" is actually a Mexican **sewer** rat.

Hidden Fears

Some stories express a common fear. For example, some experts believe that the story about the woman who adopts a Mexican dog is rooted in fears about immigration. The foreign pet seems fine until it is found to be something dangerous —a sewer rat. This story may reinforce some people's fears about people from other countries coming to the United States.

This story has been told in many different ways. In one version the "dog" looks ill, which is the reason that it is taken to the vet. The illness turns out to be rabies, and the doctor tells the woman that she is lucky that she was not bitten. The many variations make this story unlikely, but there is no proof that this story is not true.

Alligators in the Sewer

One of the most well-known urban legends is the myth of the alligators in the sewers of New York City. In this story people buy baby alligators as pets. The baby alligators are cute and harmless, but not for long. When they start to get bigger, the owners panic and flush them down the toilet. The flushed alligators end up in the sewers, where they grow to gigantic sizes.

It is also said that these alligators have eaten people. One version involving a full-grown alligator

When small pet alligators like this one grow too big to keep, careless owners may flush them down the toilet and into the sewer system, where they grow to enormous sizes and terrorize sewer workers, according to a common but untrue urban legend.

includes an **ironic** twist at the end. In this story a woman buys a baby alligator because it looks cute, but her husband objects. He tells her that the alligator will eventually grow up to be a large and dangerous animal. The woman will not listen to his reasoning and refuses to give the alligator up. The man decides he must take action. Late at night while his wife is sleeping, he flushes the alligator down the toilet. Years later the man gets a job working in the sewers. He is working with a crew deep inside a sewer when they are attacked and eaten by that same alligator.

In 1982 John T. Flaherty, the man who oversaw all the work and maintenance on the New York sewer system, had this to say about why this urban legend was most certainly untrue:

> I could cite you many cogent [convincing], logical reasons why the sewer system is not a fit habitat for an alligator, but suffice it to say that, in the 28 years I have been in the sewer game, neither I nor any of the thousands of men who have worked to build, maintain or repair the sewer system has ever seen one, and a 10-foot, 800-pound alligator would be hard to miss.[1]

The Rabbit's Revenge

Not unlike the story of the alligator eventually eating the man who flushed him, this story also in-

Harmful Habitats

Some urban legends about animals that show up where they are not supposed to be are not possible because the animal could not survive in that environment. For example, Discovery Channel's *MythBuster* Web site has this to say about alligators in the sewer: "An alligator would have difficulty surviving the cold, the close quarters, the lack of sufficient prey and the bacteria commonly found there."

MythBusters, "Myth or Fact?" http://dsc.discovery.com/fansites/mythbusters/quiz/classics/classics.html.

volves an animal getting revenge on a person who treated it cruelly. In this story two hunters who have drunk too much alcohol manage to catch a live rabbit. They decide it would be fun to strap a stick of dynamite to the poor animal's back and let it hop around until it blows up. But instead of hopping around the clearing, the scared little bunny takes cover under the hunters' brand-new pickup truck. Of course there is no way the hunters can get the rabbit to come out. As time runs out, they have no choice but to take cover and watch their truck explode. Many people find this story appealing because the hunters get just what they deserve.

Variations on an urban legend involving careless or cruel humans, innocent animals, and a stick of dynamite like this one usually end with the humans paying dearly for their bad behavior.

In another version of the story, the men are duck hunting in winter. They decide to use a stick of dynamite to blow a hole in the ice, as this will attract ducks. One man throws a stick of dynamite onto the frozen lake. Unfortunately, the hunters' dog thinks they are playing fetch. He goes after the dynamite, picks it up, and starts to bring it back to the hunters. The panicked hunters try to shoot the dog so that he will not blow them up. But they miss, and the frightened dog runs under their new truck. The dynamite blows a hole in the ice, and the wrecked truck sinks to the bottom of the lake.

Although there are people who are cruel to animals, it is unlikely that these stories are true, because they never tell the names of the hunters or the place where it happened. In addition, a frozen lake would not be strong enough to hold a large truck.

Sweaters for Penguins

Unlike the story of the cruel hunters, the penguin sweater story is one of kindness. It is also a true story. In January 2000 a tanker ship spilled 260 gallons (984L) of oil into the ocean near the southern tip of Australia. A colony of the world's smallest penguins lives on an island where the spill happened. The poor little penguins were soon covered in oil.

Rescue workers did not know what to do. The oil made it impossible for the penguins' bodies to make the natural oils that keep them warm. Many of the penguins were so sick that they could not be washed right away because the scrubbing would have killed them. They soon discovered that dressing the penguins in doll sweaters seemed to help. The sweaters kept the penguins warm until they could be cleaned. In addition, they also kept the penguins from preening, or cleaning, themselves and accidentally eating the **toxic** oil.

This penguin was one of several who were dressed in sweaters for protection when they ended up covered in oil after a spill from a ship near their habitat in Australia in January 2000.

Word soon spread through the Internet. Knitters were needed to make sweaters for penguins! The response was tremendous. Thousands of sweaters were donated. "They look so cute," said Pat Gallup, who worked with Canadian knitters. "You can just see their heads and little flippers sticking out."[2]

Frightening Food

Like animal stories, food stories are also very popular. Everyone eats, so everyone can relate to the fear of finding disgusting or dangerous things in food.

Fast-Food Freak-Outs

There are many myths about people finding disgusting things in fast food. The popular fast food chain McDonald's is often at the center of many of these stories. At various times, stories have been told about their hamburgers being made out of everything from worm meat to cow eyeballs. The cow eyeballs story was originally started because McDonald's advertised that their hamburgers were

A customer who claimed to find a finger in a bowl of Wendy's chili like the one pictured here was eventually found out to have put the finger there herself so that she could sue the company. Still, urban legends about people finding disgusting things in their fast food continue.

made from 100 percent beef. People reasoned that 100 percent meant any part of the cow was fair game to put in the burgers—even the eyeballs!

Fortunately, these stories are almost always proved false, or as in the case of the woman who found a finger in the chili—a **hoax**. In March 2005 Anna Ayala did indeed find a human finger in her chili at a California Wendy's restaurant, but she put it there herself. After a long investigation by both Wendy's and the San Jose police, the finger was found to have come from a friend of Ayala's husband who had lost it during an industrial accident. Ayala had planned to sue Wendy's for a large sum of money, but she was caught before she could file the lawsuit. "They chose the wrong city to try to victimize people and perpetrate a hoax,"[3] said San Jose police chief Rob Davis. Both Ayala and her husband went to prison for the crime. Wendy's lost millions of dollars in sales because of the incident. Unfortunately for

Targeting Big Business

Large companies are often the targets of urban legends. McDonald's, Gerber, Wal-Mart, Target, and many others have been accused of doing stupid or unethical things to sell products. This may be because attaching a well-known name to a story makes it more believable. Many people do not trust large corporations and are likely to believe stories in which the company acted unwisely.

Wendy's, most people have heard about the finger in the chili, but they have not heard that the whole thing was a hoax.

Exploding Pop Rocks

Pop Rocks candy is at the center of another popular myth. Pop Rocks was first sold in stores in 1975. The fruit-flavored candies were immediately popu-

An urban legend that claimed that eating Pop Rocks candy and drinking soda at the same time would cause a person's stomach to explode was not true, but sales of the candy still suffered for many years as a result.

lar with children because they contained a small amount of **carbonation** that would cause them to sizzle and pop when placed in the mouth. It was not long before people were claiming that mixing Pop Rocks with a Coca-Cola beverage would cause the stomach to explode.

Urban legends often take strange twists, and the Pop Rocks story is no exception. The story evolved to include a child who had been featured on a well-known TV commercial for Life cereal. The child, known as Mikey, was said to have died after eating six bags of Pop Rocks and then drinking several cans of soda. Rather than having died a horrible death, Mikey, whose real name is John Gilchrist, grew to adulthood and now works in advertising.

General Mills, the company that produced Pop Rocks, tried to dispel the stories by taking out full-page ads in newspapers across the country. But sales continued to drop. In 1983 the product was taken off the market. Another company bought the product and sold it under a different name. Today this fun and safe candy can be purchased under its original name of Pop Rocks.

Baby Food Boo-Boo

In another urban legend about food, a well-known baby food company decided to market their products in Africa. They tried to sell baby food to people in Africa using the same label they use in the United States. This label features the name of the

According to urban legend, illiterate African families assumed that the image of an infant on the label of baby food containers meant that the food inside was made from ground-up babies.

product along with the face of a baby. However, according to the legend, most people in Africa cannot read. They are used to looking at the pictures on the labels of canned goods to know what is inside. When they saw the picture of the baby, they were horrified. Rather than food for babies, they thought the jars contained ground-up babies!

While label mix-ups may happen from time to time, this story probably never did. For one thing, most Africans are not **illiterate**. About half of the people in Africa can read. Undoubtedly, this includes people who own and run the stores where the baby food is sold. In addition, many people in Africa who cannot read are also very poor and would not have enough money to buy jarred baby food. Those who could afford it most likely could also afford to go to school, where they would have learned how to read.

Bad Bananas

This urban legend, like many others, started on the Internet. In December 1999 an e-mail began circulating claiming that bananas from Costa Rica were

All over the Internet

Myths like the bacteria-infected bananas spread much quicker today than they would have ten years ago because of the Internet. When people read and believe a distressing e-mail, they want to warn their friends and family. One person may forward the e-mail to 20, 50, even 100 people.

infected with **necrotizing fasciitis**, more commonly known as flesh-eating bacteria. The e-mail warned readers about symptoms of the bacteria and what to do if they had them. It then went on to say that the government food safety organization, the Food and Drug Administration (FDA), was not going to issue a nationwide warning because it would cause mass panic. Also, the e-mail predicted that approximately 15,000 people would be affected. The e-mail claimed to be from the Manheim Research Institute.

This e-mail was a hoax, and a very good one. So many people were fooled that the Centers for Disease Control set up a special banana hotline. The bacteria does exist. It is rare, but it can cause serious damage and even death. Still, no one has ever gotten the flesh-eating bacteria from a banana or any other fruit. According to **epidemiologist** Dr. Alan Eckles: "The bacteria that most commonly causes necrotizing fasciitis lives in the human body. The FDA and CDC agree it cannot live long enough on the surface of a banana."[4] Not surprisingly, the Manheim Research Institute does not exist.

The Great Molasses Flood

This last story is more than an urban legend; it is a true story. On January 15, 1919, at 12:40 in the afternoon, a gigantic holding tank split open, sending 14,000 tons (12,500t) of molasses flowing through the streets of Boston.

Leaky Tank

The great molasses flood was caused by a broken holding tank. It was common knowledge that the tank was leaking for weeks before the tank exploded. People in the neighborhood had been using the leaks to refill their own molasses jars. The company had even painted the tank brown to help disguise the leaks.

The molasses flowed at an estimated rate of 35 miles per hour (56kph) in what eyewitnesses called "a 30 foot wall of goo."[5] The molasses destroyed buildings and tossed wagons around as if they were made from toothpicks.

By the time it was finally over, 21 people had died and 150 were seriously injured. The molasses was so sticky that it made rescue attempts nearly impossible. Author Stephen Puleo, who wrote a book about the flood, describes a devastating scene:

> Molasses, waist deep, covered the street and swirled and bubbled about the wreckage. Here and there struggled a form—whether it was animal or human being was impossible to tell. Only an upheaval, a thrashing about in the sticky mass, showed where any life was. . . .

Destruction and a gooey mess are what remained in a section of Boston, Massachusetts, after a holding tank explosion sent 14,000 tons of molasses flowing through the streets on January 15, 1919.

> Horses died like so many flies on sticky fly-paper. The more they struggled, the deeper in the mess they were ensnared [trapped]. Human beings—men and women—suffered likewise.[6]

The disaster took months to clean up, and workers may not have gotten to all of the sticky mess. Even today, there are people who claim that on hot summer days, you can still smell the molasses.

Strange and Bizarre

Strange and bizarre urban legends are often favorites. Usually they involve an exceptional amount of stupidity, kindness, or luck, both good and bad.

From the Ocean to the Fire

This urban legend is about someone who had extremely bad luck. In this story the body of a man is found draped over a charred tree branch in an extinguished forest fire. But strangely, he is in full scuba diving gear, complete with flippers, mask, and

Contrary to urban legend, it is impossible for a scuba diver such as this one to be accidentally scooped up by a firefighting helicopter's water bucket and dumped onto a forest fire.

air tank. Stranger yet, after analysis of the body, the experts say he died, not from burns, but from internal injuries. So what happened?

The man did not start off in the forest fire. On the day of the fire, he was miles away scuba diving in the Pacific Ocean. Unfortunately for him, the pilot of a firefighting helicopter accidentally scooped him up along with the water in the large bucket he was towing. The scuba diver was lifted 980 feet (300m) into the air and then dropped into the raging fire.

This is a fascinating story because it includes two favorite urban legend themes. It is both a "wrong place, wrong time" myth as well as a "dumb way to die" myth. Fortunately, this could never actually happen. Although helicopters like those in the story exist, the water only enters the buckets through small holes, about 1 foot (30cm) square.

Tanning Terrors

Even more gruesome than being dumped on a forest fire is the myth of the overly tanned woman. In this story a woman is just days from her wedding when it occurs to her that a nice tan would look good with her white dress. So she goes to a tanning salon, but the safety time limit prevents her from getting a good tan. She solves this problem by going to four more tanning salons that same day. She continues to go to several tanning salons a day until the wedding.

Although tanning beds like this one are linked to skin cancer dangers, there is no truth to the urban legend that tells of a bride tanning so much before her wedding in an effort to look good that she cooked herself from the inside out and died.

Her plan seems to have worked; she has a beautiful tan on her wedding day. But soon guests start to notice a rotting smell. No one can figure out what it is, but it seems to be coming from the bride. During the honeymoon, it gets worse. Soon after her return, the woman is found dead in her bed. The **autopsy** reveals that she had literally cooked her insides by tanning too much. The rotting smell was her organs spoiling.

This myth originated because people confused ultraviolet (sometimes called UV) waves with microwaves. Although ultraviolet waves can lead to skin cancer and burns, they do not penetrate the skin far enough to harm the organs.

The Dead Cat Thief

This story does not involve a dead human, but there is a dead cat. A woman accidentally runs over a cat. Of course she feels terrible and decides the least she can do is bury it. She does not want to carry a dead cat down the street, so she puts it in a shopping bag. While she is walking to the local park, a man suddenly runs by and snatches the bag, thinking it contains something valuable. Later, the man takes a look inside, screams, and throws up.

In another variation, a woman whose cat had just died puts it in a shopping bag to take on the bus for burial at a park. On the bus, her bag gets switched with another woman's bag, which contains a ham from the butcher. The reader is left to

A Dumb Way to Die

People dying in embarrassing, stupid, or horrific ways is a popular theme in urban legends. This may be because most people are afraid of death. Laughing at death may help people to feel less afraid. Horrific stories may be comforting because people reason that no matter how they die, it could not possibly be as bad as that poor guy in the story.

imagine what happens when the woman who thinks she has a ham in her bag finds out she does not.

It is impossible to know if these urban legends are true or not. Like many urban legends, there are no names or places given with these stories, and there are many different versions.

Generous Gestures

The next legend is about an ordinary person helping someone who seems ordinary but turns out not to be. A man is driving along a highway with his wife when he sees a **limousine** with a flat tire. He offers to help, and his assistance is happily accepted by the man in the limo. A few minutes later the tire is fixed and the man in the limo is on his way. The man does not think much about it until a few weeks later when he receives a letter from his bank. The letter informs him that billionaire Bill Gates has paid off his mortgage.

Although this story is appealing, there is no documented case of Bill Gates or any other very rich person rewarding a small favor by paying off a house. However, there is a true story of generosity involving New York City police officer Robert Cunningham. As a tip, Cunningham promised to split the winnings of a lottery ticket with his favorite waitress if he won. After his meal they each chose three

Billionaire Bill Gates exits his limousine after arriving at an event, but it's unlikely that he required the assistance of a helpful motorist to change a flat tire on his way there.

of the six numbers. Cunningham bought the ticket on his way home. The officer did indeed win—over 6 million dollars! And true to his word, he gave half to the waitress. When Cunningham's wife was asked how she felt about her husband giving away half the winnings, she replied, "Hey, she picked three of those winning numbers. She gets her half of the pot."[7] This story inspired the 1994 movie *It Could Happen to You*, starring Nicolas Cage.

Late for Choir Practice

Like winning the lottery, this true story involved a great deal of good luck. On March 1, 1950, a church in Beatrice, Nebraska, exploded due to a leak in the gas main. The explosion completely destroyed the church. The reason this story is a lucky one is because the church was empty when it exploded. It should have been filled with members of the church choir. Choir practice began at 7:20 P.M. and the explosion happened at 7:25 P.M., but on that day, all fifteen members of the choir were late for practice.

The various choir members were late for different reasons. One member had to finish her homework. Two of them had cars that would not start. One had to have her dress ironed. Another was delayed by a missionary meeting, which made her friend late, too, since they were driving together. One was writing a letter. Another reported that she was just feeling lazy and put off going until the last minute. Another was

Urban Legend Clues

Many urban legends contain flaws in the story that are often overlooked but make the story unlikely to be true. For example, in the story about the limousine with the flat tire, Bill Gates accepts help from another motorist. But what about the limousine driver? It is hard to imagine that any limo driver, especially one for Bill Gates, would not know how to change a flat tire.

delayed by talking to a friend, and he was supposed to pick up two others. One took a nap after dinner and slept too long, and her mother was late as well since they were going together. Two of them were listening to a radio program and wanted to hear the end. Every last one of the choir members was at least six minutes late, probably saving their lives.

Urban legends, whether they are true or not, are a part of our culture. Today, with the Internet, these stories are spreading faster than ever. But the Internet also makes it much easier to find out which stories are true and which are not. True or not true, it does not seem to matter. People love to tell them and people love to hear them, and they probably always will.

Notes

Chapter 2: Animal Antics

1. Quoted in Anna Quindlen, "Debunking the Myth of Subterranean Saurians," *New York Times*, May 19, 1982, p. B-3.
2. Quoted in Holly Hartman, "Penguin Sweaters: Cozy Tops Give Small Birds a Chance," Infoplease. www.infoplease.com/spot/penguinsweater. html.

Chapter 3: Frightening Food

3. Quoted in Ryan Kim and Dave Murphy, "Police Say They Know Origin of Finger in Chili. Digit Belonged to Acquaintance of Suspect's Husband." *San Francisco Chronicle*, May 13, 2005. www.sfgate.com/cgibin/article.cgi?file=/chronicle/archive/2005/05/13/finger13.TMP.
4. Quoted in David Emery, "Flesh-Eating Bananas from Costa Rica!" About.com. http://urbanlegends.about. com/library/bl bananas.htm.
5. Quoted in Ralph Frye, "The Great Molasses Flood," *Reader's Digest*, August 1955, p. 64.
6. Stephen Puleo, *Dark Tide: The Great Boston Molasses Flood of 1919*. Boston: Beacon Press, 2004, p. 98.

Chapter 4: Strange and Bizarre

7. Quoted in Lois Alter Mark, "Reality Check: Winning Personalities," *Entertainment Weekly*, July 29, 1994. www.ew.com/ew/article/0,,303110,00.html.

Glossary

autopsy: An examination of a dead body to determine the cause of death.

carbonation: Being filled or mixed with carbon dioxide.

epidemiologist: A scientist who studies the spread and control of epidemic diseases.

flammable: Easily set on fire.

hoax: An act meant to trick people into believing something is true when it is not.

illiterate: Unable to read or write.

immigration: Going to a new country in order to settle there permanently.

ironic: Involving something that is surprising or contradictory.

limousine: A large, luxurious car, usually driven by a chauffeur.

necrotizing fasciitis: The bacteria that causes flesh-eating disease.

sewer: An underground pipe that carries waste and rainwater away.

strike: An organized protest that involves employees refusing to work in order to get a specific thing, such as safer working conditions or a pay raise.

tarantula: A large, hairy spider that feeds on small animals, such as toads, lizards, and young birds.

toxic: Poisonous.

For Further Exploration

Books

Joan Hiatt Harlow, *Joshua's Song*. New York: Aladdin, 2003. This fast-paced, middle grade novel about thirteen-year-old Joshua climaxes with the Boston molasses flood of 1919.

David Holt and Bill Mooney, *The Exploding Toilet: Modern Urban Legends*. Little Rock, AR: August House, 2004. A collection of urban legends written in a short, high-interest format.

Mary Packard, *MythBusters: Don't Try This at Home*. San Francisco: Discovery Communications, 2006. Taken from the popular Discover Channel TV show, this colorful book features hosts Adam Savage and Jami Hynemann cracking fifteen myths wide open.

Web Sites

MythBusters (http://dsc. discovery.com/fansites/mythbusters/quiz/quiz.html). This is the Web site for the popular Discovery channel TV show. Features quizzes, video clips, and interesting information about the show.

The Spider Myths Site, Burke Museum of Natural History and Culture (www.washington.edu/burkemuseum/spidermyth/). This site has a wealth of information about spiders, including many myths and strange stories.

Index

A
Africa, 27–29
Alligators in sewer, 16–18, 19
Animals
  alligators, 16–18, 19
  bears, 7
  cats, 6, 36–37
  Mexican dog, 15–16
  penguins, 21–22
  pet in microwave, 5, 6
  rabbits, 18–20
  spiders, 13–15
  urban legends about, 7, 13–22
Appeal, 6, 8–11
Ayala, Anna, 25

B
Baby food, 27–29
Bananas, 29–30
Bears, 7

C
Cactus, 13–15
Cats, 6, 36–37
Choir practice, 39–40
Cunningham, Robert, 38–39

D
Dead cat thief, 36–37
Death, 37
Dynamite, 19–21

E
Eckles, Alan, 30
E-mail, 29–30

F
Fast-food stories, 23–26
Fears, 16
Firefighting helicopter, 33–35
Flaherty, John T., 18
Flammable toilet, 10–11
Flesh-eating bacteria, 30
Folktales, 11–12
Food stories
  baby food, 27–29
  bananas, 29–30
  fast-food, 23–26
  molasses flood, 30–32
  Pop Rocks, 26–27
  popularity of, 7
  restaurants, 6
Foolish behavior, 7, 9

G
Gallup, Pat, 22
Gates, Bill, 38, 40
Generous gestures, 37–39

Gerber baby food, 27–29
Gilchrist, John, 27

H
Hairdos, 11, 12
Hoaxes, 24–26, 30
Human nature, 9

I
Immigration, 16
Insects, 11
Internet, 29–30
It Could Happen to You (film), 39

L
Life cereal, 27
Lottery, 38–39

M
McDonald's, 23–24
Mexican dog, 15–16
Microwaved pet, 5, 6
Molasses flood, 30–32

N
Necrotizing fasciitis, 30

P
Penguins, 21–22
Pets, 5, 6, 15–16
Pop Rocks, 26–27
Puleo, Stephen, 31

R
Rabbits, 18–20
Rats, 15–16
Restaurants, 6
Revenge, 19–21

S
Sanitation strike, 7–8
Scorpions, 15
Scuba diver, 33–35
Sewer rats, 15–16
Sewers, 16–18, 19
Sitcoms, 9
Spiders, 13–15
Sweaters for penguins, 21–22

T
Tanning salons, 35–36
Tarantulas, 13–15
Themes, 6–8
Truth, 11–12
TV shows, 9

U
Ultraviolet waves (UV), 36
Unlikely events, 10–11
Urban legends
  about animals, 5–7, 13–22
  about food, 23–32
  appeal of, 6, 8–11
  characteristics of, 4–5
  flaws in, 40
  sources of, 5–6, 29–30
  strange and bizarre, 33–40
  themes of, 6–8
  truth of, 11–12

W
Warnings, 7
Wendy's, 24–26

Picture Credits

AP Images, 17, 22, 24, 32, 38
Michael Drager, 2008. Used under license from Shutterstock.com, 35
Al Freni/Time & Life Pictures/Getty Images, 26
Alfred Gescheidt/JupiterImages, 10
Bassam Hammoudeh/JupiterImages, 34
© iStockphoto.com/Oleg Kozlov, 8
JupiterImages, 5
James Steidl, 2008. Used under license from Shutterstock.com, 20
Justin Sullivan/Getty Images, 14
Mario Tama/Getty Images, 28
© Adrianna Williams/zefa/Corbis, 12

About the Author

As a child, Rachel Lynette occasionally dared to eat Pop Rocks and soda at the same time. She made it to adulthood without her stomach exploding and has since written over 25 books for children as well as many articles on children and family life. She has found the *Urban Legends* book to be one of the most fun books she has ever written and wishes to thank her son, David Babcock, for his invaluable help on this project. Lynette lives in the Seattle area in the Songaia Cohousing Community with her two delightful children. When she is not writing, she enjoys spending time with her family and friends, traveling, reading, drawing, inline skating, crocheting socks, and eating chocolate ice cream.